Contents

 To Learn By Video for these patterns, please visit
www.go-crafty.com/knit-101

First Things First
Getting Started

All you need to knit are needles and a few balls of yarn. One of the advantages of knitting today is the availability of a wide variety of cool little gadgets that make knitting a lot easier and even more fun. In this section, you'll find what you really need to get knitting.

Needles

Needles are obviously essential, since without them you won't be doing much knitting. There are several styles out there, all of which come in a wide variety of materials: aluminum, bamboo, even exotic woods like ebony and rosewood. Which to use depends on your project and preference; try out a few different styles until you find one that works for you.

Straight Up

Straight needles are the long, straight sticks that most of us associate with knitting. They have a point on one end and a knob on the other that keeps your stitches from sliding off the needle.

Straights are sold in pairs of various lengths, with 10" and 14" being the most common, and they'll get you through the majority of the projects you encounter.

Round About

Circular needles are shorter pointed sticks attached to one another with a length of smooth nylon cord. You can use them to knit tubular pieces (leg warmers, hats, seamless sweaters) or flat pieces.

Double Time

Double pointed needles (dpns) have points on both ends and are used to make small items in the round, turn sock heels, or make I-cords. Cable needles are double points with a U shape in the center. As you've probably guessed, they're used in cable knitting.

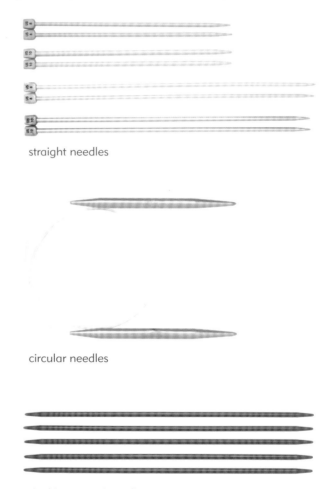

straight needles

circular needles

double pointed needles

knitting needle sizes

U.S.	Metric	U.S.	Metric	U.S.	Metric	U.S.	Metric	U.S.	Metric
0	2mm	4	3.5mm	8	5mm	11	8mm	19	15mm
1	2.25mm	5	3.75mm	9	5.5mm	13	9mm	35	19mm
2	2.75mm	6	4mm	10	6mm	15	10mm	50	25mm
3	3.25mm	7	4.5mm	10.5	6.5mm	17	12.75mm		

String Theory

Types of Yarn

Can't do much knitting without yarn, can you? The fiber choices out there are pretty staggering and a whole lot of fun to explore. Let's start with your traditional worsteds. These smooth yarns are the classic choice for sweaters; they make stitch patterns stand out and are generally the easiest for beginners to work with. Then there are the fuzzy, textured yarns like angora, mohair, bouclé (which looks like little curlicues) and chenille. You'll find them in all-natural wool, cashmere, cotton, alpaca and other animal or plant fibers; acrylic and nylon; or blends of two or more. These give lots of romantic texture, but can be a bit trickier to knit with since all that fuzz makes it harder to see your stitches. Ribbons and tapes (which tend to turn up in nylon, cotton or silk) have a flat surface that makes for a more drapey fabric. Next up are the novelties, all those fun and fabulous fake fur, eyelash, twist and combination yarns. These are great for making something incredibly simple (a garter-stitch scarf, for instance) look totally special. We also like them for accents on collars and cuffs. Like the other fuzzies, they make it a bit tricky to see stitches, but they also hide a multitude of beginner mistakes.

Various Types of Yarns

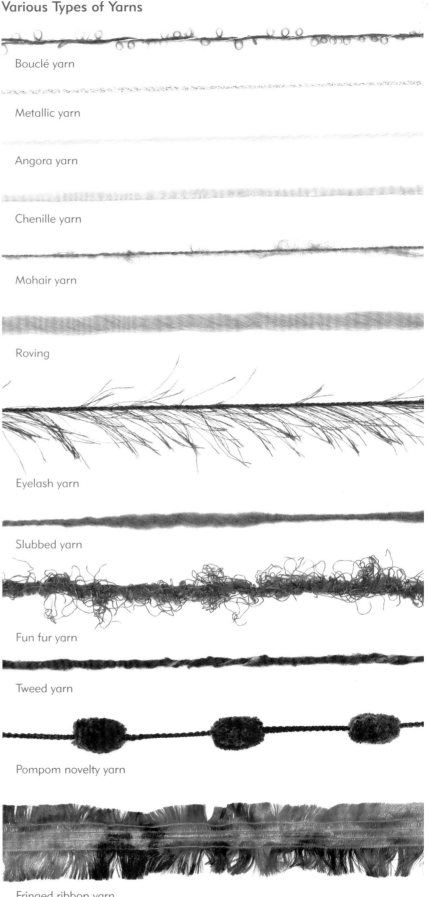

Bouclé yarn

Metallic yarn

Angora yarn

Chenille yarn

Mohair yarn

Roving

Eyelash yarn

Slubbed yarn

Fun fur yarn

Tweed yarn

Pompom novelty yarn

Fringed ribbon yarn

No matter what the fiber content, all yarns are grouped into basic categories (fingering, sport, DK, worsted, bulky, etc.) designed to help you pick the right one for your project—and your needle size. Weight (the thickness of the yarn) is the measure by which all yarns are judged, and the industry has come up with a nifty standardized list of symbols and terms to help you identify it. For the most part you'll use thinner yarns on smaller needles and thicker yarns on bigger needles. Check the ball band (the little label wrapped around your yarn) for the standardized weight symbols and information.

Standard Yarn Weight System

Categories of yarn, gauge ranges, and recommended needle and hook sizes

Yarn Weight Symbol & Category Names	1 Super Fine	2 Fine	3 Light	4 Medium	5 Bulky	6 Super Bulky
Type of Yarns in Category	Sock, Fingering, Baby	Sport, Baby	DK, Light Worsted	Worsted, Afghan, Aran	Chunky, Craft, Rug	Bulky, Roving
Knit Gauge Range* in Stockinette Stitch to 4 inches	27–32 sts	23–26 sts	21–24 sts	16–20 sts	12–15 sts	6–11 sts
Recommended Needle in Metric Size Range	2.25–3.25 mm	3.25–3.75 mm	3.75–4.5 mm	4.5–5.5 mm	5.5–8 mm	8 mm and larger
Recommended Needle U.S. Size Range	1 to 3	3 to 5	5 to 7	7 to 9	9 to 11	11 and larger
Crochet Gauge* Ranges in Single Crochet to 4 inch	21–32 sts	16–20 sts	12–17 sts	11–14 sts	8–11 sts	5–9 sts
Recommended Hook in Metric Size Range	2.25–3.5 mm	3.5–4.5 mm	4.5–5.5 mm	5.5–6.5 mm	6.5–9 mm	9 mm and larger
Recommended Hook U.S. Size Range	B–1 to E–4	E–4 to 7	7 to I–9	I–9 to K–10½	K–10½ to M–13	M–13 and larger

* GUIDELINES ONLY: The above reflect the most commonly used gauges and needle or hook sizes for specific yarn categories.

This *Standards & Guidelines* booklet and downloadable symbol artwork are available at: **YarnStandards.com**

Yarn Weights

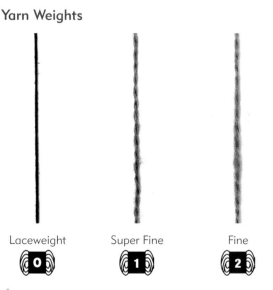

| Laceweight 0 | Super Fine 1 | Fine 2 | Light 3 | Medium 4 | Bulky 5 | Super Bulky 6 |

Tools and Accessories

Beyond yarn and a good assortment of needles, you'll need a few other tools and accessories to get yourself started. Some are more essential than others; we've broken the list down into the must-haves (The A-list) and the nice-to-haves (B-listers):

The A-list

Scissors

Whether you stick to a strictly utilitarian pair or splurge on a more decorative design (we love the little gold ones that are shaped like storks), you'll need these to cut yarn, make fringe and snip off loose ends. Pick a small pair with a sharp point that allows you to get close to the work. If you'll be doing a lot of knitting on the go, get a sleeve that protects the point or slip the scissors into a little zippered pouch so they won't poke holes in your bag—or cut your fingers when you reach in to grab them.

Yarn needles

Sometimes called tapestry needles, these have a blunt point and a wide eye (that's the little hole at the top of the needle) to accommodate thick yarn. You'll need these to sew seams and weave in ends. The metal and colorful plastic styles available work equally well.

Tape measure

You can't get your project right unless you know what size it is, so a tape measure is essential. Your basic yellow dressmaker's tape will do just fine, but many cute retractable styles exist that make measuring a little more fun. Just be sure the tape is marked in both inches and centimeters and is made of fiberglass, since cloth tends to stretch.

Ruler or stitch gauge

One or the other is essential for checking the ever-important knitting gauge. Rulers work just fine, but gauges have neat little windows that make it easier to count the number of stitches in a row. Some even have a row of holes you can use to identify the size of unmarked needles.

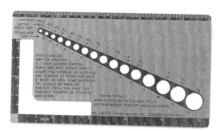

Pins

You'll need pins for seaming and blocking. You'll want a good stock of long, straight pins with glass or metal heads (plastic will melt under the heat of your iron) and T-pins for blocking. You can also purchase special blocking pins that are longer and more flexible than traditional T-pins.

Crochet hook

Every knitter needs at least one hook to help pick up stitches, make decorative edgings and seam slip stitches.

Stitch holders

Slip open stitches (like those on a neckline) onto these oversized safety pins to keep them from unraveling until you are ready to pick them up again.

Stitch markers

These little plastic or metal rings are handy for keeping track of things like where to increase and decrease or the beginning of a circular row. Split markers have a little slit in the ring so you can slip the marker into the stitches instead of over the needle.

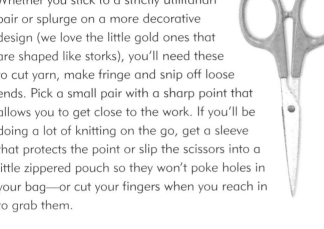

NECESSITY IS THE MOTHER OF INVENTION

Stuck short without the tool you need? Try these substitutes:

Stitch holder Thread stitches onto a length of fishing line or cording and tie the ends.

Point protectors Push the needle tips into erasers or wrap rubber bands around the points.

Cable needle A skinny pencil makes a nice substitute; just take care that yarn doesn't snag on the metal that holds the eraser.

Stitch markers Tie short pieces of yarn into little loops and slipover your needles (a contrasting color will work best).

Knitting tote Is this an essential? Probably. You'll need a spot for storing your stuff, and while your old backpack or a plastic grocery sack will do the job just fine, it's kind of nice to have a beautiful bag to tote around town. The best knitting totes have multiple pockets for needles and accessories and offer easy access to your work-in-progress.

B-Listers

These aren't essential, but they will make your knitting life easier:

Pompom makers

These little plastic disks work like magic to create perfectly plush and perky pompoms. Follow the directions on the package to get the best results.

Point protectors

These are little rubber pointed covers you put over the points of your needles to keep stitches from falling off. They also prevent needles from poking holes in your bag. They are available in lots of sizes, shapes and colors.

Bobbins

When you do colorwork, wind yarn around these little plastic holders, using them like small-scale balls of yarn. They help prevent tangles and make it easier to work the design.

Needle cases

Like knitting bags, these little accessories have exploded in style and popularity. Some are simple plastic zippered cases, others are artfully designed rolls crafted from silk or other fab fabrics. Look for one with loops to hold hooks and needles and a flap or zippered closure to keep them from spilling out.

Notebook

It's a good idea to keep a record of what you've made and how you did it. You can use a simple spiral-bound notebook to keep track of your progress, or splurge on one of the many knitting journals offering space to record everything from yarn and needle inventories to your thoughts on what you're knitting and why you're knitting it.

Learn to Knit

Getting those first stitches on the needle is actually harder than knitting, but we'll get you through it.

Okay, so you have your yarn, you have your needles and you're ready to start stitching— almost. Before you really get into the knitting groove, you have to create a foundation row for all those stitches. Doing this is called "casting on," and it all starts with a little something called a slip knot.

This little loop is where it all begins. Let's get started....

The Slip Knot

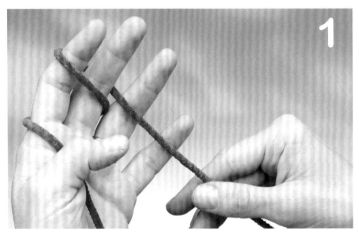

1 Hold the short end of the yarn in your palm and use your thumb to hold it in place. Wrap the yarn twice around the index and middle fingers.

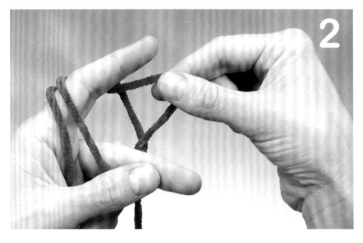

2 Pull the strand attached to the ball through the loop between your two fingers, forming a new loop.

3 Place the new loop on the needle. Tighten the loop on the needle by pulling on both ends of the yarn to form the slip knot.

TIP

If you're a newbie, you may cast on so tightly that when it comes time to knit you find it difficult to get the needle into the little loops. To loosen up, try casting on with a needle two sizes larger than the one you'll be using for the rest of the project. If on the other hand, your stitches come out too loose and droopy, using a needle two sizes smaller should tighten things up.

Casting On

Knitting, you'll soon discover, is all about choices. And the cast-on, that foundation row from whence all stitches start, can be accomplished using several different methods. Which one you decide to use is mostly a matter of preference.

We're going to show you two of the most basic: the double cast-on (also known as the long tail cast-on), which uses one needle and two lengths of yarn, and the knit-on cast-on, which uses two needles and one strand of yarn.

Double Cast-on How-to

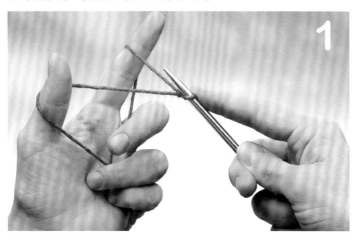

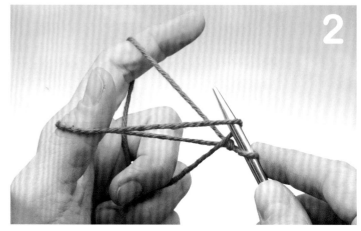

1 Make a slip knot on the right needle, leaving a long tail. Wind the tail end around your left thumb, front to back. Wrap the yarn from the ball over your left index finger and secure the ends in your palm.

2 With us so far? Good. Now insert the needle upward in the loop on your thumb.

3 Then with the needle, draw the yarn from the ball through the loop to form a stitch.

4 Take your thumb out of the loop and tighten the loop on the needle. Continue in this way until the correct number of stitches is cast on.

Knit-on Cast-on How-to

1 Make a slip knot on the left needle. *Insert the right needle from front to back into the loop on the left needle.

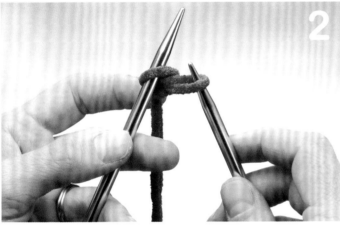

2 Wrap the yarn around the right needle in a clockwise motion. Draw the yarn through the first stitch to make a new stitch, but don't drop the stitch from the left needle.

3 Slip the new stitch to left needle, just like the photo shows. Repeat from the * in Step 1 until the required number of stitches are cast on.

That wasn't so bad, was it? Practice makes perfect so keep casting on until you feel comfortable with the technique and your stitches look neat and even.

The Knit Stitch

Got your cast-on down? Good. Now you are ready to learn to knit. But first you have to decide if you'll be using the English or the Continental method. Both are easy to do and will achieve the same end result, so just pick the one that seems most comfortable. Here's how to get started:

English Method

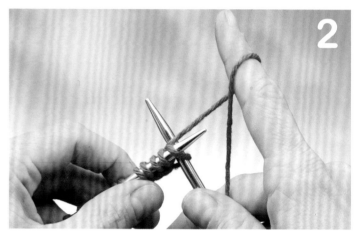

1 Hold the needle with the cast-on stitches in your left hand. Hold the empty needle in your right hand, and wrap the yarn tail around your index finger. Slip the right needle from front to back into the loop on the left needle. Keep the right needle under the left and the yarn at the back.

2 Wrap the yarn over and under the right needle in a clockwise motion.

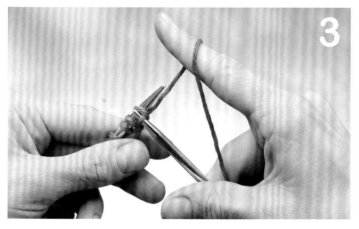

3 With the right needle, catch the yarn and pull it through the cast-on stitch.

4 Slip the cast-on stitch off the left needle, leaving the newly formed stitch on the right needle. Repeat these steps in each subsequent stitch until all stitches are off the left needle. Ta-da! You've made one row of stitches.

Garter Stitch

Your first row is complete, but one row does not make a sweater or scarf! If you want your stitches to shape up into something usable, you're going to have to keep going. Here's where we introduce you to garter stitch, that most basic of all stitch patterns. All you do is knit every row and you'll end up with a flat, reversible ridged fabric that looks like this:

It's ultra-easy to do. Really. Here's how it works. When you get to the end of your first row of knit stitches, just switch the needles in your hands. Now the needle with the stitches on it is in your left hand and the empty needle is in your right. Start knitting each stitch again (following steps 1 to 4 of either the English or the Continental method as show above and on the next page). It may look a little wonky at first, but after a few rows you'll have something that really resembles a strip of fabric. Pretty cool, huh?

Continental Method

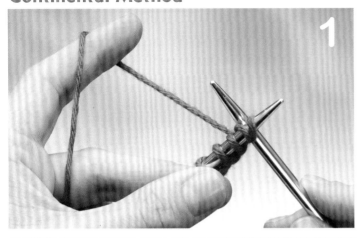

1 Hold the needles as described in Step 1 of the English method (opposite), but hold the yarn with your left hand rather than your right. Insert the right needle from front to back into the first cast-on stitch on the left needle. Keep the right needle under the left, with the yarn in back of both needles.

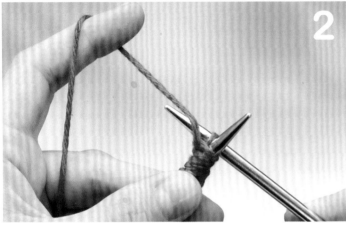

2 Lay the yarn over the right needle as shown.

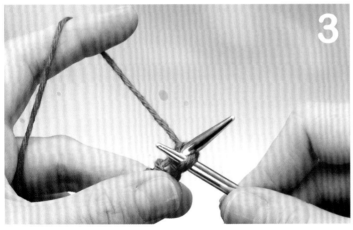

3 With the tip of the right needle, pull the strand through the cast-on stitch. Use your right index finger to hold the strand if you need to.

4 Slip the cast-on stitch off the left needle, leaving the newly formed stitch on the right needle. Repeat these steps until you've transferred all of the stitches from the left needle to the right. You've just completed one row of stitching.

Purling

Garter stitch is great, but to really experience all of knitting's creative possibilities you need to take the next step and learn to purl. Purling is really just a backward version of knitting. Put the two together and you can create hundreds of different stitch patterns.

The Purl Stitch

Some people find purling a bit more awkward than knitting (that's why we showed you how to knit first), but with practice you should find it just as easy to do. As with the knit stitch, you can take your pick from two methods of purling: English or Continental, whichever you're most comfortable with.

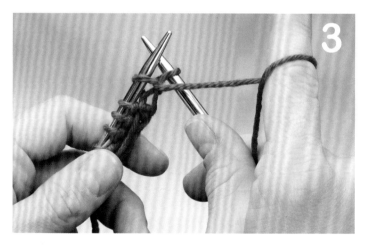

English Method

1 Hold the needle with the cast-on stitches in your left hand and the empty needle in your right. Put the tail of the yarn in front of the needle. Insert the right needle from the back to front into the first stitch on the left needle.

2 The right needle is now in front of the left needle and the yarn is at the front of the work. With your right index finger, wrap the yarn counterclockwise around the right needle.

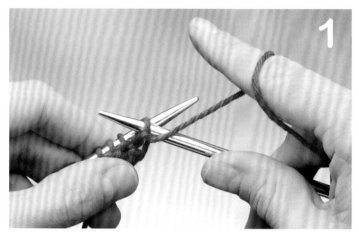

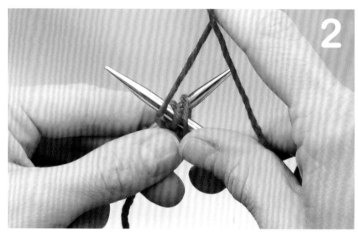

3 Draw the right needle and the yarn backward through the stitch on the left needle, forming a loop on the right needle.

4 Slip the stitch off the left needle. You have made one purl stitch. Repeat these steps until all of the stitches are off of the left needle. You've made one row of purl stitches.

Continental Method

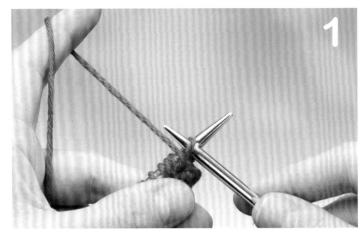

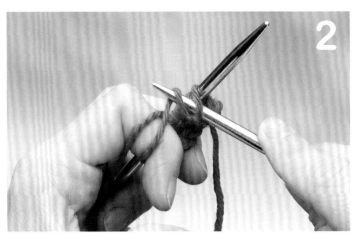

1 Hold the needle with the cast-on stitches in your left hand and the empty needle in your right (just as you did for knitting). This time, however, the tail of the yarn goes in front of the needle. Insert the right needle from back to front into the first stitch on the left needle, keeping the yarn in front of the needle.

2 Lay the yarn over the right needle as shown. Pull down on the yarn with your left index finger to keep it taut.

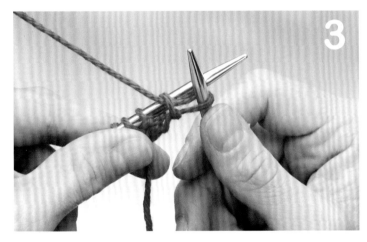

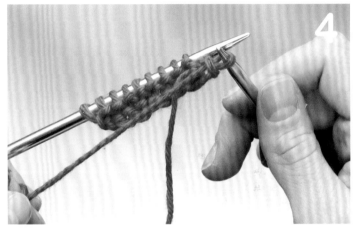

3 Bring the right needle and the yarn backward through the stitch on the left needle, forming a loop on right needle.

4 Slide the stitch off the left needle. Use your left index finger to tighten the new purl stitch on the right needle.

Continue to repeat these steps until you have worked all of the stitches from the left needle to the right needle. You have made one row of purl stitches.

Stockinette Stitch

Once you've learned how to knit and purl you can put the two together to form that V-patterned fabric most people associate with knitting: the stockinette stitch. How, you ask? Easy, we say. You simply knit one row, then purl the next, alternating every row until you have a piece of knitting that looks like this:

Let's Talk about Texture:
Ribs and Other Textured Stitches

As we mentioned earlier, knit and purl stitches can be combined in many different ways to create all kinds of cool, textural patterns. To do this, switch back and forth between knit and purl stitches within the same row.

Ribbing

Ribbing is one of the most widely used knit and purl combinations. Since the pattern is very stretchy, it's found most often on sweater hems, cuffs and necks. Used in the main body of a sweater, it creates a body-hugging fabric.

Ribbing is also incredibly easy to do. In the most basic form, you knit one stitch, purl the next and keep alternating until you reach the end of the row.

The other great thing about ribbing is that once you've done a row or two, you can put down your instructions and let the stitches show you what to do. Knit the stitches that look like a "v" and purl the ones that look like a bump. The tricky part is remembering to move the yarn from back to front and front to back as you make the different knit and purl stitches. If you don't, you'll end up with extra stitches on the needle and a very lumpy-looking rectangle. The pictures on the right should make things clearer.

When knitting a stitch, the yarn is always held at the back of the work. When you purl, the yarn is held in the front. With us so far? When you are working the rib, remember to make sure that the yarn is in the correct position to work the next stitch.

For a knit 1, purl 1 rib, for example, you would knit the first stitch keeping the yarn to the back of the work. Before you purl the next stitch, slip the yarn between the needles (not over them!) and bring it to the front of the work.

Yarn in back   **Yarn in front**

Seed stitch

This is another easy stitch that adds lots of great texture to your project. It starts out like a rib: for the first row (which will be the right side of your fabric), you'll follow a knit 1, purl 1 pattern across the row. But on the second row, you'll follow a purl 1, knit 1 pattern. In the end, you'll get a bumpy little surface that looks like this:

Seed stitch
(Over an even number of sts)
Row 1 (RS) *K1, p1; rep from * to end.
Row 2 *P1, k1; rep from * to end.
Rep rows 1 and 2.

Moss stitch

For this ultra easy stitch, simply alternate ribbed rows with rows that are knit straight across.

Moss stitch
(Multiple of 2 sts plus 1)
Rows 1 and 3 (RS) Knit.
Row 2 P1, *k1, p1; rep from * to end.
Row 4 K1, *p1; k1; rep from * to end.
Rep row2 1–4.

Basketweave

Basketweave combines knit and purl stitches to create a fabric that looks like—you guessed it—a woven basket (hence the name). It's great for scarves and pillows, but you can use it pretty much anywhere. Here's how it looks:

Basketweave
(Multiple of 8 sts plus 5)
Row 1 (RS) Knit.
Row 2 K5, *p3, k5; rep from * to end.
Row 3 P5, *k3, p5; rep from * to end.
Row 4 Rep row 2.
Row 5 Knit.
Row 6 K1, *p3, k5; rep from *, end last rep k1.
Row 7 P1, *k3, p5; rep from *, end last rep p1.
Row 8 Rep row 6.
Rep rows 1–8.

There are lots of variations to the stitches we've shown you here (k2, p2 ribs, double seed stitch, for example), plus a whole slew of other patterns. If you are interested in exploring even more stitches, get yourself a stitch dictionary, which provides pictures of many different stitches along with instructions for how to create them.

Getting into Shape

Increases and Decreases

Unless you want to spend the rest of your knitting career stitching squares and rectangles, you'll need to learn how to increase and decrease stitches. This is a simple matter of subtracting and adding stitches from and to the needle, so that you can add and subtract inches to the knitted piece. There are a number of ways to do this; we're going to show you a few of the most common. Let's start with two decreases: Knit two together and purl two together (k2tog and p2tog).

k2tog

Insert the right needle from front to back (knitwise) into the next two stitches on the left needle. Wrap the yarn around the right needle (as when knitting) and pull it through. You have decreased one stitch.

p2tog

Insert the right needle into the front loops (purlwise) of the next two stitches on the left needle. Wrap the yarn around the right needle (as when purling) and pull it through. You have decreased one stitch.

Bar increase

The bar increase is made by working into the front and back loop of the same stitch. It leaves a small, slightly visible bar that you can hide in a seam or embrace as a design element. Here's how to do it:

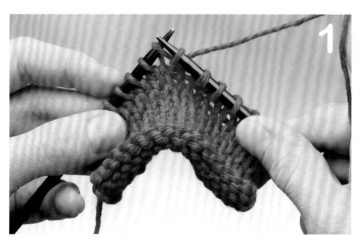

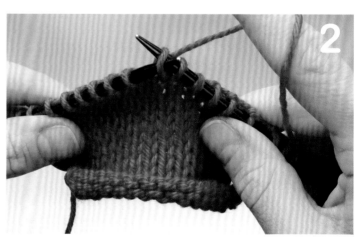

1 Insert the right needle knitwise into the stitch to be increased. Wrap the yarn around the right needle and pull it through as if to knit, but leave the stitch on the left needle.

2 Insert the right needle into the back loop of the same stitch. Wrap the yarn around the needle and pull it through. Slip the stitch off the left needle. You have increased one stitch.

Beyond the Basics:
Yarn Overs and Cables

Now that you are knitting and purling your way through all sorts of projects and patterns, let's up the ante by introducing techniques a little (but only a little!) more complicated: yarn overs and cables.

Yarn Overs

Yarn overs are increases that leave a little hole in your knitting. Yarn overs make lovely lace or eyelet patterns. Here's how they work:

Yarn over by bringing the yarn from the back of the work to the front between the two needles. Knit the next stitch, bringing the yarn to the back over the right needle.

TIP
First-timers often forget and drop the extra stitch created by the yarn over on the next row. Make sure you knit or purl the stitch as the pattern requires.

Cables

Cables are those beautiful winding, rope-like designs we all associate with fisherman's sweaters and preppy crew necks. To make cables, you will need a small, double-pointed needle called a cable needle. Cable needles work as placeholders for stitches you need to come back to. By knitting "out of order," we can create an intriguing twisted effect. Most cables are worked as knit stitches over a purl background, and many come with a chart. Try knitting this cable:

Giant Cables

Right cable
(panel of 16 sts)
12-st right cable Sl 6 sts to cn and hold to back of work, k6, k6 from cn.
Rows 1 and 3 (RS) P2, k12, p2.
Row 2 and all WS rows K the knit sts and p the purl sts.
Row 5 P2, 12-st right cable, p2.
Row 7 Rep row 1.
Row 8 Rep row 2.
Rep rows 1–8.

Left cable
(panel of 16 sts)
12-st left cable Sl 6 sts to cn and hold to front of work, k6, k6 from cn.
Rows 1 and 3 (RS) P2, k12, p2.
Row 2 and all WS rows K the knit sts and p the purl sts.
Row 5 P2, 12-st left cable, p2.
Row 7 Rep row 1.
Row 8 Rep row 2. Rep rows 1–8.

All Things Bright and Beautiful:
Working with Color

You haven't exactly been knitting in black and white, but up to this point, the scene has been a bit monotone. So let's work on livening things up with an introduction to colorwork.

Show Your Stripes

Stripes are the easiest way to introduce a little color into your knitting. Basically, you just knit a few rows to the width you want, then change to a new color when you're ready for a different stripe. (For info on how to do this, see "Joining Yarn" on page 23). There's no complicated color changing mid-row, and you can simply carry the colors along the side when you switch to a new stripe. You'll see how simple this is below:

Carrying colors along the side

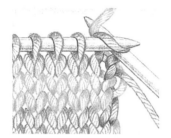

1 When changing colors with narrow, even-numbered stripes, drop the old color. Bring the new color under the old color, being sure not to pull the yarn too tightly, and knit the next stripe.

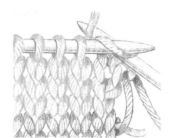

2 When working thicker stripes (generally more than four rows), carry the old yarn up the side until it is needed again by twisting the working yarn around the old yarn every couple of rows, as shown.

Fair Play

Fair Isle, also known as stranded knitting, takes its name from the remote British Isle where the style developed. Many moons ago, the local women started stitching great geometrically patterned designs that were doubly warm, thanks to the strands of wool carried across the back of the sweater as the patterns were knit.

These days the term refers to any kind of colorwork characterized by small repeated patterns, and it's a lot easier to accomplish than it looks. Multiple colors are used in the design, but only two colors are used in any one row. As you stitch across the row, you use only the color called for in the pattern and carry the other color loosely across the back. Watch and learn as we explain in more detail:

Stranding

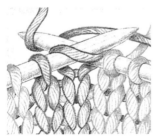

1 On the knit side, drop the working yarn. Bring the new color (now the working yarn) over the top of the dropped yarn and work to the next color change.

2 Drop the working yarn. Bring the new color under the dropped yarn and work to the next color change. Repeat steps 1 and 2.

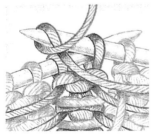

3 On the purl side, drop the working yarn. Bring the new color (now the working yarn) over the top of the dropped yarn and work to the next color change.

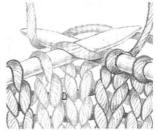

4 Drop the working yarn. Bring the new color under the dropped yarn and work to the next color change. Repeat steps 3 and 4.

If you are going to be working more than four stitches between color changes, it's advisable to weave or twist the color not being used into or under the stitches. If you don't do this, you risk catching the long, loose floats on fingers, jewelry, belly rings or belt buckles. Here's how:

Weaving above a knit stitch

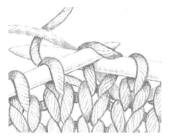

1 Hold the working yarn in your right hand and the yarn to be woven in your left. To weave the yarn bring it over the right needle. Knit the stitch with the working yarn, bringing it under the woven yarn.

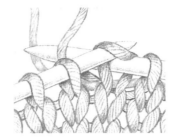

2 The woven yarn will go under the next knit stitch. With the working yarn, knit the stitch, bringing the yarn over the woven yarn. Repeat steps 1 and 2 to the next color change.

Weaving above a purl stitch

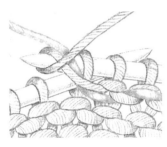

1 To weave the yarn on the purl side, bring it over the right needle. Purl the stitch with the working yarn, bringing it under the woven yarn.

2 To weave the yarn below a purl stitch, purl the stitch with the working yarn, bringing it over the woven yarn. Repeat steps 1 and 2 to the next color change.

Twisting

1 On the knit side, twist the working yarn and the carried yarn around each other once. Then continue knitting with the same color as before.

2 On the purl side, twist the yarns around each other as shown, then continue purling with the same color as before.

TIP
When working more than two colors across the row, the yarns can easily get tangled. To avoid this, wind bobbins or create little butterflies (see photo on page 55). You will find that untangling these smaller balls is much easier than balls of yarn.

Picture This: Intarsia

Now on to intarsia, which involves large blocks of single colors worked with separate balls of yarn. These can create a picture (heart, flower, pirate skull, or what ever else strikes your fancy), or an abstract or geometric design.

Since the designs are worked over large areas, it's not practical to carry yarn across the back of the work (you'd end up with a tangled mess, not to mention waste a lot of yarn), so you use separate balls (or bobbins) of yarn for each large block of color and twist the different colors around each other at each color change to prevent holes.

Allow us to demonstrate:

Changing colors in a vertical line

1 On the knit side, drop the old color. Pick up the new color from under the old color and knit to the next color change.

2 On the purl side, drop the old color. Pick up the new color from under the old color and purl to the next color change. Repeat steps 1 and 2.

Changing colors in a diagonal line when working a right diagonal

1 On the knit side, bring the new color over the top of the old color and knit to the next color change.

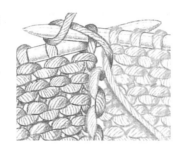

2 On the purl side, pick up the new color from under the old color and purl to the next color change.

Changing colors in a diagonal line when working a left diagonal

1 On the purl side, bring the new color over the top of the old color and purl to the next color change.

2 On the knit side, pick up the new color from under the old color and knit to the next color change.

TIP
When changing colors, always twist the yarns on the wrong side to prevent holes in the work.

Joining a new color: Version A

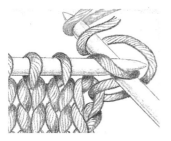

1 Wrap first the old and then the new yarn knitwise and work the first stitch with both yarns.

2 Drop the old yarn. Work the next two stitches with both ends of the new yarn.

3 Drop the short end of the new color and continue working with the single strand. On the following rows, work the three double stitches as single stitches.

Joining a new color: Version B

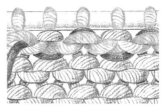

1 Cut the old yarn, leaving about 4 inches (10cm). Purl the first two stitches with the new yarn. *Insert the needle purlwise into the stitch, lay the short ends of both the old and new colors over the top of the needle, and purl the next stitch under the short ends.

2 Leave the short ends hanging and purl the next stitch over them.

3 Repeat from the * until you have woven the short ends into the wrong side of the piece.

Joining a new color: Version C

1 Work to three stitches before where you want to join the new yarn. Work these stitches with the yarn folded double, making sure you have just enough to work three stitches.

2 Loop the new yarn into the loop of the old yarn, leaving the new yarn doubled for about 8 inches (20cm). Knit the next three stitches with the doubled yarn. Let the short end of the new yarn hang and continue knitting with one strand.

3 On the next row, carry the first yarn across the back of the work from where it was dropped on the previous row and twist it together with the second yarn. Work the doubled stitches as single stitches.

Going in Circles

Knitting in the Round

Getting a little tired of doing everything on the straight and narrow? We're going to throw you a curve here with an introduction to knitting in the round.

This means instead of working back and forth as you do with straight needles, you simply keep knitting (or purling) in a spiral of sorts, creating a tube rather than a flat piece of knitting. To do this you are going to need those circular needles we discussed earlier.

Circulars can be found in several lengths. You'll need to choose one that is long enough to hold all of your stitches, but short enough so the stitches are not stretched when joined. (Don't stress too much about this—your pattern instructions will tell you how long the needles need to be.) Cast on your stitches just as you would for straight knitting, taking care not to twist the stitches. (If you do, your fabric will end up twisted, too.) The last stitch you cast on will be the last stitch in your round. Place a marker over the needle so you'll know where the round ends, and start knitting as shown below:

TIP
If the plastic or nylon cord connecting your circular needles gets curled, immerse it in hot water to work out the kinks.

1 Hold the needle tip with the cast-on stitch in your right hand and the tip with the first cast-on stitch in your left hand. Knit the first cast-on stitch, pulling the yarn tight to avoid a gap.

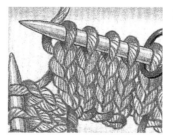

2 Work until you reach the marker. This completes the first round. Slip the marker to the right needle and work the next round.

As you join rounds, make sure the stitches are not twisted. Keeping the cast-on edge facing the center will help keep things straight.

TIP
Circular needles can also be used for "flat" knitting. You simply flip the work over at the end of a row and continue stitching.

Joining Yarn and Binding Off

Joining Yarn

When you finish a ball of yarn and need to continue, all you need to do is join a new ball of yarn. Try to do this at the end of a row, even if it means cutting off some of the yarn from the previous ball. This will make it easier to weave in the ends later and the stitches won't be distorted. Here's how:

Joining yarn at the end of a row

Tie the yarn from the new ball loosely around the old, leaving a six-inch tail. Untie the knot later and weave the ends into the seam. If you must join a new ball mid-row, use this method:

Joining yarn mid-row

1 Insert the right needle into the next stitch to be worked, wrap the new yarn around the right needle and start knitting with the new yarn.

2 Work to the end of the row. Tie the old and new strands together loosely before continuing so they will not unravel

Binding Off

At some point all good things must come to an end. Once your knitted fabric is the length you want it to be, you'll stop knitting and start binding off. Binding off gets the stitches off the needle and keeps them from unraveling. To bind off:

1 Knit two stitches. *Insert the left needle into the first stitch on the right needle.

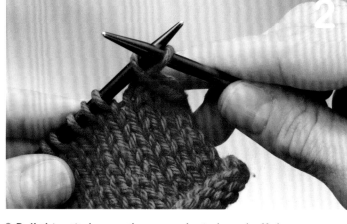

2 Pull this stitch over the second stitch and off the right needle.

Continue binding off by repeating from the * in step 1 until you have bound off all but one stitch. Carefully slip that stitch off the needle and pull the tail of the yarn through the loop. Remember to take it easy as you do this. Binding off too tightly (a common beginner's mistake) will make the edges pucker, something that won't add any beauty points to your work. If you find your bind-off is too tight, try using a needle a size or two larger than the one used in the project to loosen things up.

3 One stitch remains on the right needle as shown here. Knit the next stitch.

Gauge

Knitting gauge—the number of rows and stitches per inch—determines the size of the garment (or bag, or blanket) you are making. It's also one of the most important factors in your knitting. Every pattern states the gauge on which the sizing for the project is based (in the U.K. they call it "tension"). If you don't get it right from the get-go, you risk ending up with a garment that doesn't fit. And since everything from the size and brand of the needles you're using to how loosely or tightly you knit can affect your gauge, you should always, always, always test your knitting against the pattern gauge before you begin the project. How do you do this? Simple. You make a gauge swatch. Basically this is just a square piece of knitted fabric that demonstrates how you, the needles and the yarn all work together. Start by gathering up the exact yarn and needles you intend to use for the project. Cast on enough stitches to create a square at least 4 inches wide— anywhere from 12–20 depending upon the size of the needles and the thickness of the yarn you are using should do it. Then knit or work in the specified stitch pattern until the square is a little more than 4 inches high.

Slip the stitches off the needle (no need to bind off unless you really want to) and put the swatch down on a table or other smooth, hard surface.

1 Use a tape measure or ruler to measure 4 inches across the swatch. Count the number of stitches in those 4 inches. Compare this number to the stitches given in the stated gauge.

2 Using the same ruler or tape, measure from the bottom to the top of the swatch and count the number of stitches in those 4 inches. This will give you the number of rows.

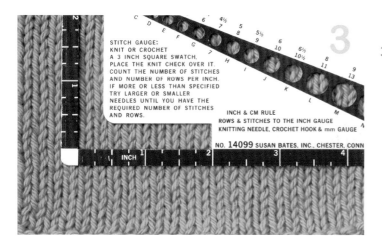

STITCH GAUGE:
KNIT OR CROCHET
A 3 INCH SQUARE SWATCH.
PLACE THE KNIT CHECK OVER IT.
COUNT THE NUMBER OF STITCHES
AND NUMBER OF ROWS PER INCH.
IF MORE OR LESS THAN SPECIFIED
TRY LARGER OR SMALLER
NEEDLES UNTIL YOU HAVE THE
REQUIRED NUMBER OF STITCHES
AND ROWS.

INCH & CM RULE
ROWS & STITCHES TO THE INCH GAUGE
KNITTING NEEDLE, CROCHET HOOK & mm GAUGE
NO. 14099 SUSAN BATES. INC., CHESTER, CONN

3 If you're a gadget geek, use a stitch gauge to get the same results. Place the gauge on your swatch and count the stitches that appear in the window.

Compare these numbers to those in the gauge given for your pattern. If they match, you are ready to get started. If they don't, you'll have to change your needle size and try again. If you were short a few stitches, try using smaller needles. If you had too many stitches, try using larger needles. (As a general rule, larger needles give fewer stitches to the inch, smaller needles give more.) Try different needle sizes until you get the correct gauge. Checking and adjusting your knitting is important. If your knitting is as much as a half an inch off from the recommended gauge, you can end up with a HUGE difference in the size of your finished garment. It's also a good idea to recheck your gauge once you have about 5 inches or so completed on the actual project.

For those of you still questioning the necessity of knitting a gauge swatch, take a gander at this comparison of two gauge swatches.

Both swatches have exactly the same number of stitches and rows, but the one on the left was stitched with needles one size smaller than the one on the right. Now repeat after us: "I will knit a gauge swatch for every project I undertake, always and without exception."

Terms and Abbreviations

At first glance, knitting instructions can look like some weird form of code: "Cast on 22 sts. *k1, p2 rep from *." Those weird-looking strings of letters, numbers and symbols are part of a system of knitting terminology used to save space and make instructions easier to read. K1, for instance, simply means knit one stitch. Rep from * means to repeat the instructions after the asterisk as many times as indicated. Sts stands for stitches. The glossary below will help you get you through your projects.

abbreviations

approx	approximately
beg	begin, beginning
cont	continue
dec	decrease
foll	follow(s)
in/cm/mm	inches/centimeters/millimeters
inc	increase
inc(dec) sts evenly across row	Count the number of stitches in the row, and then divide that number by the number of stitches to be increased (decreased). The result of this division will tell you how many stitches to work between each increased (decreased) stitch.
k the knit and p the purl sts	This is a phrase used when a pattern of knit and purl stitches has been established and will be continued for some time. When the stitch that's facing you looks like a V, knit it. When it looks like a bump, purl it.
k	knit
k2tog	knit two together (a method of decreasing explained on page 52)
k3tog	knit three together. Worked same as k2tog, but insert needle into three sts instead of two for a double decrease.
knitwise	Insert the needle into the stitch as if you were going to knit it.
oz/g	ounces/grams (usually in reference to amount of yarn in a single ball)
p	purl
p2tog	purl two together (a method of decreasing explained on page 52)
pat	pattern
pm	place marker
purlwise	Insert the needle into the stitch as if you were going to purl it.
sk2p	Slip one, knit two together, pass slipped stitch over k2tog
rem	remain, remains or remaining

rep	repeat
rep from *	Repeat the instructions after the asterisk as many times as indicated. If the directions say "rep from * to end," continue to repeat the instructions after the asterisk to the end of the row.
rev sc	reverse single crochet
reverse shaping	A term used for garments such as cardigans where shaping for the right and left fronts is identical, but reversed. For example, neck edge stitches that were decreased at the beginning of the row for the first piece will be decreased at the end of the row on the second. In general, follow the directions for the first piece, being sure to mirror the decreases (increases) on each side.
RS	right side
sc	single crochet
SKP	Slip one stitch knitwise to right-hand needle. Knit the next stitch and pass the slipped stitch over the knit stitch.
slip	Transfer the indicated stitches from the left to the right needle purlwise without working (knitting or purling) them.
Small (Medium, Large)	The most common method of displaying changes in pattern for different sizes. In general, the measurements, stitch counts, directions, etc. for the smallest size come first, followed by the increasingly larger sizes in parentheses. If there is only one number given, it applies to all of the sizes.
ssk	On RS, slip next two stitches knitwise. Insert tip of left needle into fronts of these two stitches and knit them together. On WS, slip one stitch, purl one stitch, then pass slip stitch over purl stitch.
st/sts	Stitch/stitches
St st	stockinette stitch
tog	together
work even	Continue in the established pattern without working any increases or decreases
WS	wrong side
yo	yarn over

All Together Now:
Making Your First Sweater

Sizing and Construction

Enough stitch talk for now. Let's discuss how to make sure your sweaters shape up the way they should.

Follow the Instructions

We recommend that you read through an entire pattern before you cast on a single stitch. Circle or highlight the information that pertains to your size and look up any unfamiliar terms or abbreviations before you start. Reading through the instructions before starting helps you to plan ahead before you start to knit.

Size matters

Most patterns patterns provide instructions for the smallest size, with larger sizes given in parentheses: S (M, L), for example: if the pattern says to cast on 43 (44, 46) sts, that means you would cast on 43 stitches for a size Small, 44 stitches for a size Medium and 46 stitches for a size Large. Highlighting or circling the numbers that pertain to your size will make it easier to follow the pattern. Knitting a garment can take weeks or even months to complete, so the last thing you want to discover is that the garment is two sizes too large (or worse, too small). Make sure you are happy with the fit of your project by paying close attention to the measurements given in the pattern. To size yourself up against the pattern, stand in your undies and measure around the fullest part of your chest. If you are knitting a skirt, shorts or dress, you'll also need to measure around your hips (at the widest part) and natural waistline (to find this, tie a piece of string around your middle and see where it falls). As you measure, hold the tape snug, but not tight—and don't cheat. Giving yourself a few inches more or less won't get you a garment that fits properly. Compare the bust/chest measurement in the pattern to your own measurements, remembering that the numbers given in the pattern refer to the finished size of the garment. Choose the size with the bust (for sweaters) or hip (for skirts) measurement that comes closest to your own. (Choose dresses by bust size, as it is easier to alter at the hips if you need to.) You may want to measure a sweater you like that is similar in style to the one shown in the pattern and use it as a guide for picking your size.

The scheme of things

Toward the end of many sweater patterns you'll find a mini representation of the sweater's pieces, called a schematic. Drawn to scale, these little line illustrations are labeled with the name (back, sleeve, left front, etc.) and the exact measurements of the piece. They also allow you to see the shape of the item you are about to make. If you've followed the instructions correctly, your knit pieces will look just like the picture when you've finished. Here's what your average schematic for a simple sweater looks like:

6 (6½, 6¾)"
7½ (8, 8¾)"
23 (23½, 24¼)"
15½"
17 (18½, 20)"
FRONT & BACK

7½ (8, 8¾)"
13½ (14½, 15½)"
18 (18½, 19)"
8½ (8½, 9)"
SLEEVES

The numbers preceding the parentheses represent the measurements for the smallest size; those inside indicate measurements for sequentially increasing sizes. For a cardigan, the schematic will usually show just one of the two fronts, and you'll have to imagine a mirror image for the other.

Women's Sizing

Woman's size	X-Small	Small	Medium	Large	1X	2X	3X	4X	5X
Bust (in.) cm.)	28–30 71–76	32–34 81–86	36–38 91.5–96.5	40–42 101.5–106.5	44–46 111.5–117	48–50 122–127	52–54 132–137	56–58 142–147	60–62 152–158
Center Back Neck-to-Cuf	27–27½ 68.5–70	28–28½ 71–72.5	29–29½ 73.5–75	30–30½ 76–77.5	31–31½ 78.5–80	31½–32 80–81.5	32½–33 82.5–84	32½–33 82.5–84	33–33½ 84–85
Back Waist Length	16½ 42	17 43	17¼ 43.5	17½ 44.5	17¾ 45	18 45.5	18 45.5	18½ 47	18½ 47
Cross Back (Shoulder to Shoulder	14–14½ 35.5–37	14½–15 37–38	16–16½ 40.5–42	17–17½ 43–44.5	17½ 44.5	18 45.5	18 45.5	18½ 47	18½ 47
Sleeve Length to Underarm	16½ 42	17 43	17 43	17½ 44.5	17½ 44.5	18 45.5	18 45.5	18½ 47	18½ 47
Upper arm	9¾ 25	10¼ 26	11 28	12 30.5	13½ 34.5	15½ 39.5	17 43	18½ 47	19½ 49.5
Armhole depth	6–6½ 15.5–16.5	6½–7 16.5–17.5	7–7½ 17.5–19	7½–8 19–20.5	8–8½ 20.5–21.5	8½–9 21.5–23	9–9½ 23–24	9½–10 24–25.5	10–10½ 25.5–26.5
Waist	23–24 58.5–61	25–26½ 63.5–67.5	28–30 71–76	32–34 81.5–86.5	36–38 91.5–96.5	40–42 101.5–106.5	44–45 111.5–114	46–47 116.5–119	49–50 124–127
Hips	33–34 83.5–86	35–36 89–91.5	38–40 96.5–101.5	42–44 106.5–111.5	46–48 116.5–122	52–53 132–134.5	54–55 137–139.5	56–57 142–144.5	61–62 155–157

Measuring up

The schematic also helps you to make sure the measurements of your finished knit pieces match those given in the pattern instructions. To see how your pieces are shaping up as you knit, lay the piece out on a flat, smooth surface and, using a tape measure, take the measurement in the middle of a row. Determine the length of your work by measuring from the row below your needle to the bottom edge. When measuring the length of an armhole, don't measure along the curve or slanted edge—if you do the measurement will be inaccurate. Instead, measure in a straight line from the needle to the first armhole decrease.

Block party

Before you're ready to stitch your sweater together you'll need to block (which is just a knitty way of saying soak or steam) the pieces into shape. This is one rather tedious step that is tempting to skip. DON'T. Blocking is to knitting as pressing or ironing is to sewing. Without it, your perfectly knit project will look sloppy and homemade—and not in a good way.

There are two kinds of blocking: wet and steam. To determine which you should use with your yarn, check out our handy blocking guide. For wet blocking, immerse the pieces in cool water, squeeze them out between two towels, shape them on an ironing board or pressing pad (a folded towel will also do) and pin them to their exact measurements, or pin first and use a spray bottle to dampen the fabric. Then leave 'em alone until they are completely dry. For steam blocking, pin the pieces to their measurements on your board, then fire up your iron to steam. Hold the iron close to the fabric (don't actually touch the pieces with the iron) and steam away until everything is nice and damp. As with wet blocking, you'll leave the pieces to dry.

BLOCKING GUIDE

Because fibers react differently to heat, it is best to know what to expect before you block or steam them. Just remember that there are many combinations of fibers, and you should choose a process that is compatible with all the components of your yarn. If you are unsure about the fiber content of your yarn, test your gauge swatch before blocking your sweater pieces.

Angora	Wet block by spraying.
Cotton	Wet block or warm/hot steam block.
Linen	Wet block or warm/hot steam block.
Lurex	Do not block.
Mohair	Wet block by spraying.
Novelties	Do not block.
Synthetics	Carefully follow instructions on ball band—usually wet block by spraying. Do not press.
Wool and all wool-like fibers (alpaca, camel hair, cashmere)	Wet block by spraying or warm steam block.
Wool blends	Wet block by spraying. Do not steam unless tested.

Just sew

Okay, so you have all the pieces for your sweater finished and blocked to perfect size. It's time to put them together to create the garment (or bag, or whatever else you are making).

Things will go easier if you assemble the pieces as follows:
1 Seam the shoulders.
2 Finish the neck edge (the pattern instructions will tell you how to do this).
3 Sew the sleeves to the body of the sweater.
4 Sew continually from the end of the sleeve to the underarm and then down the body of the sweater to the bottom edge.

Our handy sweater map shows you how it all fits together and explains what you need to do to prepare each piece. Nice, huh?

To actually join the pieces together, you're going to need a tapestry needle and yarn. Line up the pieces by finding the cast-on stitches on both sides. Use pins to hold them together. Next, count up about 10 rows on each side and pin the corresponding stitches together. Keep at it until you reach the tops of the two pieces. On projects worked all in one piece (a hat or tube top, for instance), the rows should line up exactly. If they don't, go back and see where you slipped up. When you are pinning two separate pieces (a sweater back and front, for example) you may have to ease in extra rows if one piece is slightly longer than the other. Once you have everything pinned, you can begin seaming using one of the following methods.

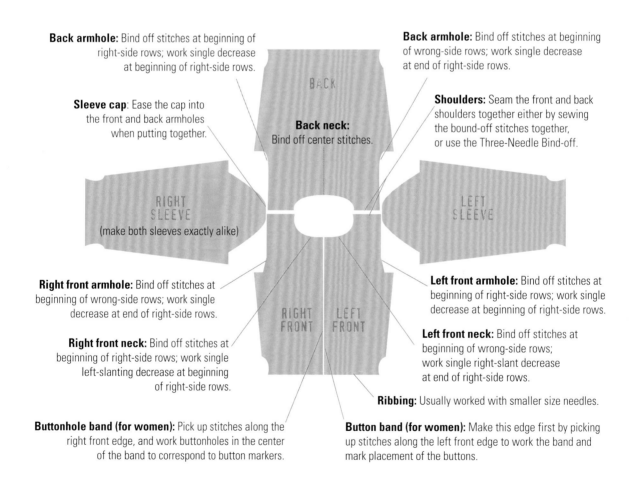

Back armhole: Bind off stitches at beginning of right-side rows; work single decrease at beginning of right-side rows.

Sleeve cap: Ease the cap into the front and back armholes when putting together.

Back neck: Bind off center stitches.

Back armhole: Bind off stitches at beginning of wrong-side rows; work single decrease at end of right-side rows.

Shoulders: Seam the front and back shoulders together either by sewing the bound-off stitches together, or use the Three-Needle Bind-off.

BACK

RIGHT SLEEVE
(make both sleeves exactly alike)

LEFT SLEEVE

RIGHT FRONT

LEFT FRONT

Right front armhole: Bind off stitches at beginning of wrong-side rows; work single decrease at end of right-side rows.

Right front neck: Bind off stitches at beginning of right-side rows; work single left-slanting decrease at beginning of right-side rows.

Left front armhole: Bind off stitches at beginning of right-side rows; work single decrease at beginning of right-side rows.

Left front neck: Bind off stitches at beginning of wrong-side rows; work single right-slant decrease at end of right-side rows.

Ribbing: Usually worked with smaller size needles.

Buttonhole band (for women): Pick up stitches along the right front edge, and work buttonholes in the center of the band to correspond to button markers.

Button band (for women): Make this edge first by picking up stitches along the left front edge to work the band and mark placement of the buttons.

Seaming

How to begin seaming

If you have a long tail left from your cast-on row, you can use this strand to begin sewing. To make a neat join at the lower edge with no gap, use the technique shown here.

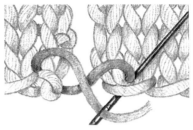

Thread the strand into a yarn needle. With the right sides of both pieces facing you, insert the yarn needle from back to front into the corner stitch of the piece without the tail. Making a figure eight with the yarn, insert the needle from back to front into the stitch with the cast-on tail. Tighten to close the gap.

Vertical seam on stockinette stitch

The vertical seam is worked from the right side and is used to join two edges row by row. It hides the uneven stitches at the edge of a row and creates an invisible seam, making the knitting appear continuous. Insert the yarn needle under the horizontal bar between the first and second stitches. Insert the needle into the corresponding bar on the other piece. Continue alternating from side to side.

Vertical seam on garter stitch

This seam joins two edges row by row, like vertical seaming on stockinette stitch. The alternating pattern of catching top and bottom loops of the stitches ensures that only you can tell there's a join.

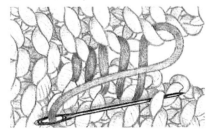

Insert the yarn needle into the top loop on one side, then in the bottom loop of the corresponding stitch on the other side. Continue to alternate in this way.

Vertical seam on ribbing
Knit to knit

When joining ribbing with a knit stitch at each edge, insert the yarn needle under the horizontal bar in the center of a knit stitch on each side in order to keep the pattern continuous.

Purl to purl

When joining ribbing with a purl stitch at each edge, use the bottom loop of the purl stitch on one side and the top loop of the corresponding purl stitch on the other side.

Horizontal seam on stockinette stitch

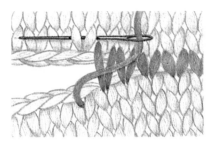

This seam is used to join two bound-off edges, as for shoulder seams or hoods, and is worked stitch by stitch. Each piece must have the same number of stitches so that the finished seam will resemble a continuous row of knit stitches. Be sure to pull the yarn tightly enough to hide the bound-off edges.

With the bound-off edges together, and lined up stitch for stitch, insert the yarn needle under a stitch inside the bound-off edge of one side and then under the corresponding stitch on the other side. Repeat all the way across the join.

Vertical to horizontal seam

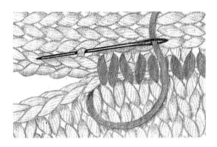

Used to connect a bound-off edge to a vertical length of knitted fabric, this seam requires careful pre-measuring and marking to ensure an even seam. Insert the yarn needle under a stitch inside the bound-off edge of the vertical piece. Insert the needle under one or two horizontal bars between the first and second stitches of the horizontal piece (opposite on stockinette stitch).

Slip-stitch crochet seam

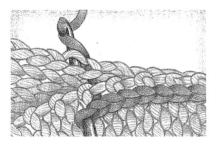

This method creates a visible, though very strong, seam. Use it when you don't mind a bulky join or are looking for an especially sturdy connection.

With the right sides together, insert the crochet hook through both thicknesses. Catch the yarn and draw a loop through. *Insert the hook again. Draw a loop through both thicknesses and the loop on the hook. Repeat from *, keeping the stitches straight and even.

Backstitch

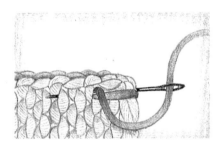

The backstitch creates a strong, neat, bulky seam that's perfect for extra reinforcement. With the right sides of the pieces facing each other, secure the seam by taking the needle twice around the edges from back to front.
Bring the needle up about ¼"/5mm from where the yarn last emerged, as shown.

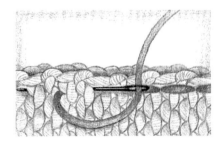

In one motion, insert the needle into the point where the yarn emerged from the previous stitch and back up approximately ¼"/5mm ahead of the emerging yarn. Pull the yarn through. Repeat this step, keeping the stitches straight and even.

The Finish Line:
Final Touches

Most of the styles we've shown you have what are called self finishing edges, meaning that your cast-on or bind-off row serves as the edge of your neckline, cuff or hem. But for some projects you'll need to take things a step further, picking up stitches to add a collar, cuff, button band or border. And, of course, if you are adding a button band, you are going to need some buttonholes to go with it. Let see how it's all done, shall we?

Pick-Me-Ups

Picking up stitches simply means that you'll use a needle or crochet hook to dip a new strand of yarn in and out of the edge of your knitting fabric, creating new loops to serve as the foundation row for your collar, button band or whatever else the pattern calls for. It's very easy to do, as long as you keep two things in mind: 1. Make sure you start picking up with the right side facing out, and 2. Space those new stitches evenly across the fabric. Here's how it's done:

Picking up on vertical edge with knitting needle

1 Insert the knitting needle into the corner stitch of the first row, one stitch in from the side edge. Wrap the yarn around the needle knitwise.

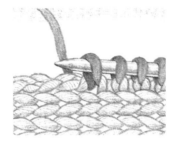

2 Draw the yarn through. You have picked up one stitch. Continue to pick up stitches along the edge. Occasionally skip one row to keep the edge from flaring.

Picking up on horizontal edge with crochet hook

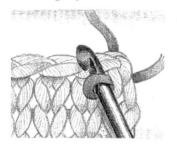

1 Insert the crochet hook from front to back into the center of the first stitch one row below the bound-off edge. Catch the yarn and pull a loop through.

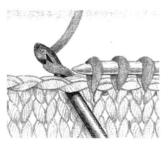

2 Slip the loop onto the knitting needle, being sure it is not twisted. Continue to pick up one stitch in each stitch along the bound-off edge.

Curved Edges

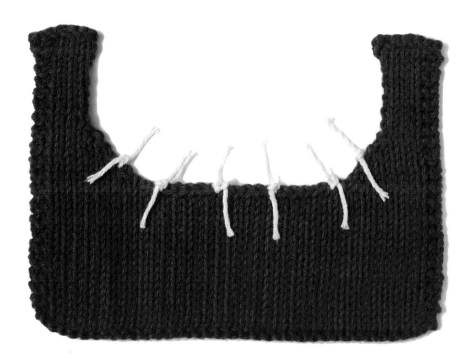

When you pick up stitches on a curved edge (necklines are a good example) you'll have to be even more careful with the spacing and number of stitches you pick up. Too many and the band will flare out, too few and it will pull in. We explain below:

Marking edge for picking up stitches

Stitches must be picked up evenly so that the band will not flare or pull in. Place pins, markers or yarn, as shown above, every 2"/5cm, and pick up the same number of stitches between each pair of markers. If you know the number of stitches to be picked up, divide this by the number of sections to determine how many stitches to pick up in each one. If you don't have a final count, use the marked sections to ensure even spacing around the neck.

Picking up stitches along a shaped edge

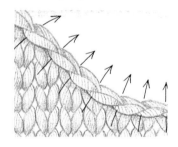

Pick up stitches neatly just inside the shaped edge, following the curve and hiding the jagged selvage.

Picking up stitches along a diagonal edge

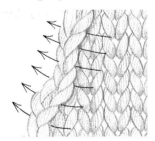

Pick up stitches one stitch in from the shaped edge, keeping them in a straight line.

Button Up!

If your coat or cardigan will close with buttons, you're going to need a few openings to slip them through. Start by placing markers (you can use pins or little pieces of yarn) on the button band for the first and last buttonhole, then measure the distance between and space the remaining markers accordingly. Got that done? Good. Now let's move on to creating the buttonholes themselves.

We're going to show you two of the easiest techniques for picture-perfect buttonholes, starting with the most common, the two-row horizontal style. This one is nice because you can easily make it larger or smaller. To create it, you simply bind off a number of stitches on one row, then cast them on again on the next, like so:

two-row horizontal buttonhole

1 On the first row, work to the placement of the buttonhole. K2, pull the 2nd st on right needle over the first st, *K1, pull 2nd st over first st; rep from * twice more. Four stitches have been bound off.

2 On the next row, work to the bound-off stitches and cast on four stitches using backward loop cast on as follows: wrap yarn around left thumb from front to back and insert right needle into the loop on thumb. Slip loop to right needle and pull to tighten.

one-row horizontal buttonhole

Slightly more difficult to execute is the one-row horizontal buttonhole. But since it's nice, neat, and very sturdy we think it's worth the extra effort.

1 Work to the buttonhole marker, bring yarn to front and slip one stitch purlwise. Move yarn to back and leave it there. *Slip next stitch from left needle. Pass the first slipped stitch over; repeat from the * three times more (not moving yarn). Slip the remaining stitch to left needle and turn work.

2 Cast on five stitches as follows, using cable cast-on with the yarn in back: *Insert the right needle between the first and second stitches on the left needle, draw up a loop, place the loop on the left needle; repeat from the * four times more, turn the work.

3 Slip the first stitch with the yarn in back from the left needle and pass the extra cast-on stitch over it to close the buttonhole. Work to the end of the row.

Once your buttonhole is in place, you can sew on the buttons. To get the holes and the buttons to line up correctly, count the number of rows between the lower edge and the first buttonhole, between the first and second hole, and so on. Then place markers for buttons on the corresponding rows of the button band. Use yarn or matching thread and a tapestry needle to stitch the buttons in place. Double the yarn and knot the ends, then slip your button onto the needle and stitch it to the fabric.

Fluff Piece

Pompoms

Ahh, the pompom. Plump, plush and ever so perky. Here's how to make a perfect one. You can use pompoms as a decorative trim, at the ends of cords, on hats or hoods, and for children's garments. They are easy to make.

1 With two circular pieces of cardboard the width of the desired pompom, cut a center hole. Then cut a pie-shaped wedge out of the circle.

2 Hold the two circles together and wrap the yarn tightly around the cardboard. Carefully cut around the cardboard between the two halves.

3 Tie a piece of yarn tightly between the two circles. Remove the cardboard and trim the pompom.

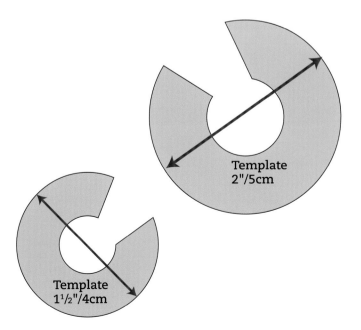

Template 2"/5cm

Template 1½"/4cm

Fringe Benefits

Fringe and tassels work up fast and fabulous. Depending on the type of yarn and where you use it, the look can be cowboy cool or showgirl sassy. We're big fans of both.

Simple fringe Cut yarn twice the desired length plus extra for knotting. Fold a cluster of strands (between 2 and 4) in half. On the wrong side, insert the hook through the piece and over the folded yarn. Pull the fold in the yarn through. Draw the ends through the loop and tighten. Trim the yarn.

Knotted fringe After working a simple fringe (it should be longer to account for extra knotting), take half of the strands from each fringe and knot them with half the strands from the neighboring fringe.

Tassels

Tassel Wrap yarn around cardboard the length of the tassel, leaving a 12"/30cm strand loose at either end. With a yarn needle, knot both sides to the first loop and run the loose strand under the wrapped strands. Pull tightly and tie at the top. Cut the lower edge of the tassel and, holding the tassel about ¾"/2cm from the top, wind the top strands (one clockwise and one counterclockwise) around the tassel. Thread the two strands and insert them through the top of the tassel.

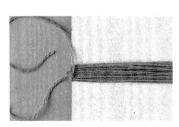 

Easy Projects
to Get You
Started

Garter Stitch Scarf

Yarn 4
Worsted Weight Yarn 1¾oz/50g hanks, each approx 77yd/70m
1 hank each in
aqua (A), chartreuse (B), icy citrine (C), turquoise (D), icy aqua (E) and green grass (F)

Needles
One pair size 8 (5mm) needles or size to obtain gauge

LEARN BY VIDEO
www.go-crafty.com
- Cast on
- K (knit)
- Bind off
- Pom poms

Measurements
4 x 48"/10 x 122cm (without pom poms)

Gauge
18 sts and 34 rows to 4"/10cm over garter st using size 8 (5mm) needles.
Take time to check gauge.
Note Always end each 4"/10cm stripe with a WS row so that color change is visible on WS only.

Scarf
With A, cast on 18 sts. *Cont with A, work in garter st (knit every row) for 4"/10cm, ending with a WS row. Work 4"/10cm stripes with B, C, D, E and F; rep from * once more. Bind off.

Finishing
Make 2 pom poms each in colors A, B, D and F as foll: wind yarn around two fingers about 15 times. Cut yarn and remove from fingers. Tie a 12"/30.5cm piece of yarn tightly around middle of pom pom. Cut loops and trim ends so that pom pom measures ½"/1.5cm. Sew one of each color to each end of scarf.

Baby Hat

Yarn 3
DK Weight Yarn 1¾oz/50g
skeins, each approx177yd/107m
1 skein in teal or coral

Needles
One set (5) size 6 (4mm)
double-pointed needles
(or size to obtain gauge

Notions
Stitch marker

LEARN BY VIDEO
www.go-crafty.com
• Cast on
• P (purl)
• K (knit)
• k2tog (knit two
  stitches together)
• I-cord
• Bind Off

Sized for 1 (2,3) years

Measurements
Head circumference 13 (14½, 16)"/33
(37,40.5)cm

Gauge
22 sts and 28 rows to 4"/10cm over
St st using size 6 (4mm) needles.
Take time to check gauge.

Hat
Cast on 72 (80, 88) sts. Divide sts
evenly over 4 needles—18 (20, 22) sts
on each needle. Join, taking care not
to twist sts. Place marker for beg of rnd
and sl marker every rnd.
Knit 8 rnds.

Beg ridge pat
[Purl 4 rnds, knit 4 rnds] 3 times.
Purl 4 rnds. Cont in St st (k every rnd)
to end of hat as foll: Knit 2 rnds.

Top shaping
For size 3 years only
Next dec rnd [K9, k2tog] 8 times
—80 sts.
Knit 1 rnd.

For sizes 2 (3) years only
Next dec rnd [K8, k2tog] 8 times
—72 sts.
Knit 1 rnd.

For all sizes
Next dec rnd [K7, k2tog] 8 times
—64 sts.
Knit 1 rnd.
Next dec rnd [K6, k2tog] 8 times
—56 sts.
Knit 1 rnd.
Next dec rnd [K5, k2tog] 8 times
—48 sts.
Knit 1 rnd.

Next dec rnd [K4, k2tog] 8 times
—40 sts.
Knit 1 rnd.
Next dec rnd [K3, k2tog] 8 times
—32 sts.
Knit 1 rnd.
Next dec rnd [K2, k2tog] 8 times
—24 sts.
Knit 1 rnd.
Next dec rnd [K1, k2tog] 8 times
—16 sts.
Next 2 rnds *K2tog; rep from *
around.
Slip rem 4 sts to 1 dpn.

I-cord knot
***Next rnd** Knit 4. Slide sts to beg of
needle to work next rnd from RS. Rep
from * until I-cord measures approx
3½"/9cm. Bind off. Tie cord in a knot.

Ribbed Fingerless Mitts

Yarn
Worsted Weight yarn,
4.16oz/118g hanks, each
approx. 225yd/206m
1 hank each in ime (MC)
and periwinkle (CC)

Needles
One pair each sizes 7 and 8
(4.5 and 5mm) needles
or size to obtain gauge
One set (4) double-pointed
needles (dpn) size
7 (4.5mm) for thumb

Notions
Stitch marker

LEARN BY VIDEO
www.go-crafty.com
• Cast-on
• K (knit)
• P (purl)
• Bind Off

Measurements
Circumference approx 6¾ (7½)"/17
(19)cm*
***Note** due to the elasticity of the
ribbing the mitts will pull in or stretch
to fit.
Length with cuff unfolded
11¼"/28.5cm

Gauge
20 sts and 22 rows to 4"/10cm over k2,
p2 rib, slightly stretched, using size 7
(4.5mm) needles.
Take time to check gauge.

P2, K2 RIB
(multiple of 4 sts plus 2)
Row 1 (RS of cuff, WS of main body)
P2, *k2, p2; rep from * to end.
Row 2 K2, *p2, k2; rep from * to end.
Rep rows 1 and 2 for k2, p2 rib.

Cuff
With larger needles and CC, cast on 34
(38) sts loosely in CC and larger needle.
Purl 1 row on WS. Change to MC.
Work in k2, p2 rib until piece measures
3¾"/9.5cm from beg.

Main body
Change to smaller needles and cont in
rib until piece measures 11"/28cm from
beg, end with a RS row. Change to CC
and purl 1 row on WS. Bind off loosely
in rib.
Work a second mitt in same way.

Finishing
Sew side seams as foll: With RS of cuff
facing (with p2 at edges), beg at cast-
on edge and using mattress st, sew cuff
seam for 3¾"/9.5cm, turn piece inside
out so that edge sts are now k2 and
cont seaming from RS of main body for
4½ (4)"/11.5 (10)cm. Skip 1½ (2)"/4
(5)cm for thumb opening and sew rem
1½"/4cm to end of piece.

Thumb
With RS facing, 3 dpn and MC, pick up
and k 12 (16) sts evenly around thumb
opening. Join to work in the rounds.
Next rnd *K2, p2; rep from * to end
of round. Rep last rnd for 5 rnds more.
Cut MC, join CC and knit 1 rnd. Bind
off loosely.

Soft Cowl

Yarn 5
Chunky Weight Yarn
7.05oz/200g hanks
each approx. 160yd/146m
2 hanks in aqua

Needles
Size 19 (15mm)
circular needle, 24"/60cm long
or size to obtain gauge

Notions
Stitch marker

LEARN BY VIDEO
www.go-crafty.com
• Cast on
• K (knit)
• P (purl)
• Rnds (rounds)
• Bind Off

Measurements
Circumference approx 32"/81.5cm
Length approx 15½"/39.5cm

Gauge
6 sts and 9 rnds to 4"/10cm over pat st using size 19 (15mm) needle and 2 strands of yarn held tog.
Take time to check gauge.

Pattern Stitch
(multiple of 4 sts)
Rnd 1 *K2, p2; rep from * around.
Rnd 2 Knit.
Rep rnds 1 and 2 for pat st.

Cowl
With 2 strands of yarn held tog, cast on 48 sts.

Join to work in rnds, taking care not to twist sts on needles. Place marker for beg of rnd and sl marker every rnd. Purl 1 rnd. Knit 1 rnd. Purl 1 rnd. Work in pat st until piece measures 14"/35.5cm from beg, end with a pat rnd 2. Purl 1 rnd. Knit 1 rnd. Purl 1 rnd. Bind off sts loosely knitwise.

Plant Cozies

Yarn (4)

Worsted Weight Yarn
3oz/85g balls, each
approx 197 yds/180m
1 ball each in
(A) Delft Blue
(B) Spring Green
(C) Seaspray
(D) Turquoise
(E) Lilac

Needles

One pair size 8 (5mm) needles
or size to obtain gauge

LEARN BY VIDEO
www.go-crafty.com
• Cast On
• inc (increase)
• K (knit)
• P (purl)
• Bind Off

Measurements

Small cozy is 12"/30.5cm around by 2¼"/6cm high.
Large cozy is 17"/43 cm around by 5½"/14cm high.

Gauge

16 sts and 25 rows to 4"/10cm over St st using size 8 (5mm) needles.
Take time to check gauge.

Make the Small Cozy

2-color version

With Spring Green, cast on 38 sts. Working in stripe pat of [2 rows Spring Green, 2 rows Turquoise] 3 times, 2 rows Spring Green, work as foll:
Work in St st for 2 rows.
Next (inc) row (RS) K1, inc 1 st in next st, k to last 2 sts, inc 1 st in next st, k1. Purl 1 row. Rep last 2 rows 4 times more—48 sts. Work 2 rows even. Bind off purlwise on RS.

Rainbow-colored version

With Delft Blue, cast on 38 sts. Working shaping as for the 2-color style, work stripes as foll: Work 3 rows Delft Blue, 2 rows Lilac, 2 rows Turquoise, 2 rows Spring Green, 2 rows Seaspray, 2 rows Delft Blue, 1 row Lilac. Bind off purlwise on RS with Lilac.

Make the Large Cozy

With Delft Blue, cast on 60 sts. Work in St st for 2 rows.
Next (inc) row (RS) K1, inc 1 st in next st, k to last 2 sts, inc 1 st in next st, k1. Purl 1 row. Rep the last 2 rows 13 times more—88 sts. Work in St st for 2 rows. Bind off purlwise on RS.

Finish the Cozies

Sew the short edges of cozy together to form the tube that fits around the flowerpot.

Ribbed Hat & Scarf

Scarf

Yarn

Worsted Weight Yarn
1¾ oz/50g skeins,
each approx. 125 yd/114m
7 skeins each in navy (A)
and denim heather (B)

Needles

One set (4) size 8 (5mm) dpns
or size to obtain gauge

LEARN BY VIDEO
www.go-crafty.com
• Cast on
• Sl k-st with yo
  (Slip Knit Stitch
  with Yarn Over)
• Sl p-st with yo
  (Slip Purl Stitch
  with Yarn Over)
• K2tog (knit two
  together)
• Yo tog (yarn over
  together)
• Dec (decreasing)
• Pm (place marker)
• Bind off

Measurements

Width approx 14"/35.5cm
Length 78"/198cm

Gauge

33 sts and 32 rows to 4"/10cm over slip
st rib, laid flat without stretching, using
size 8 (5mm) needles.
Take time to check gauge.

Slip Stitch Rib

(multiple of 4 sts plus 3)
Row 1 (RS) *K3, bring yarn to front
between needles, sl 1 purlwise, bring
yarn to back between needles; rep from
*, end k3.
Row 2 K1, bring yarn to front between
needles, sl 1 purlwise, bring yarn to
back between needles, *k3, bring yarn
to front between needles, sl 1 purlwise,
bring yarn to back between needles; rep
from *, end k1.
Rep rows 1 and 2 for sl st rib.

Side A

With A, cast on 59 sts. Work in sl st rib
for 78"/198cm. Bind off in pat.

Side B

With B, cast on 59 sts. Work in sl st rib
for 78"/198cm. Bind off in pat.

Finishing

With RS of each side facing and cast-on
edges at lower edge, sew the two long
sides tog.

Hat

Yarn
Worsted Weight Yarn
1¾ oz/50g skeins,
each approx. 125 yd/114m
2 skeins each in blue"

Needles
Size 7 (4.5mm) circular needle,
16"/40cm long or size to
obtain gauge
One set (4) size 7(4mm) dpns

Notions
Stitch marker

Sized for Small (Medium/Large).

Measurements

Brim circumference (unstretched)
19¾ (22)"/50 (56)cm
Length 8½ (9)"/21.5 (23)cm

Gauge

13 sts and 20 rnds to 4"/10cm over
brioche rib, slightly stretched, using size
7 (4.5mm) needles.
Take time to check gauge.

Stitch Glossary

Sl 1 k-st with yo With yarn at front, sl
next k st purlwise to RH needle, wrap
yarn over RH needle and around to
front again.

Sl 1 p-st with yo With yarn at front, sl
next p st purlwise to RH needle,wrap
yarn over RH needle to back for yarn
over, ready to work next knit st.

2-st decrease K2tog (next knit st with
yarn over tog with foll p st), slip st back
to LH needle, pass the foll k st with
yarn over on LH needle over st and off
needle, slip st back to RH needle
—2 sts dec'd.

With circular needle, cast on 64 (72)
sts. Join, taking care not to twist sts on
needle. Place marker (pm) for beg of
rnd and sl marker every rnd.
Set-up rnd *K1, sl 1 p-st with yo; rep
from * around.
Rnd 1 *Sl 1 p-st with yo, k next st and
yo tog; rep from * around.
Rnd 2 *P next st and yo tog, sl 1 k-st
with yo; rep from * around.
Rep rnds 1 and 2 until cap measures
6½"/16.5cm from beg, end with a rnd 2.

Shape crown

Note Change to dpns when there
are too few sts to fit comfortably
on circular needle.
Place a marker on every 8th (9th) knit
rib—4 markers placed.
Next (dec) rnd [Work in pat to knit
rib before marked knit rib, work 2-st
decrease] 4 times—8 sts dec'd.
Rep dec rnd every 4th rnd 2 (3) times,
then every other rnd once—32 sts.
Work 1 rnd even.
Next rnd (dec) [Sl 1 p-st with yo, 2-st
decrease] 8 times—16 sts.
Cut yarn leaving a long tail. Thread
through rem sts, draw up and secure.

Textured V-Neck

Yarn

Worsted Weight Yarn
1¾ oz/50 g hanks,
each approx. 109yd/100m
5 (6, 7, 7, 8) balls in russet

Needles

Size 8 (5mm) circular needles
20"/50cm long or size to
obtain gauge

Notions

Stitch holder
Stitch markers

LEARN BY VIDEO
www.go-crafty.com
- Cast on
- K (knit)
- P (purl)
- Wyib (with yarn in back)
- Wyif (with yarn in front)
- Bind Off
- pm (place marker)
- sl marker (slip marker)
- k2tog (knit two sts together)
- rnds (rounds)

Sized for Small (Medium, Large, 1X, 2X)

Measurements

Bust 36 (40, 44, 48, 52)"/91.5 (101.5, 111.5,122, 132)cm
Length 22 (22½, 23½, 24, 25)"/56 (57, 59.5, 61, 63.5)cm
Upper arm 14 (15, 16, 17, 18)"/35.5 (38, 40.5, 43, 45.5)cm

Gauge

24 sts and 40 rows to 4"/10cm over garter slip st using size 8 (5mm) needles. *Take time to check gauge.*

K1, P1 Rib

(multiple of 2 sts plus 1)
Row 1 (RS) K1, *p1, k1; rep from * to end.
Row 2 P1, *k1, p1; rep from * to end.
Rep rows 1 and 2 for k1, p1 rib.

Garter slip stitch

(multiple of 2 sts plus 1)
Rows 1 and 2 Knit.
Row 3 (RS) K1, *sl 1 purlwise wyib, k1; rep from * to end.

Row 4 K1 , *sl 1 purlwise wyif, k1; rep from * to end.
Rep rows 1–4 for garter slip st.

Back

Cast on 109 (121, 133, 145, 157) sts. Work in k1, p1 rib for 1"/2.5cm, end with a WS row. Work in garter slip st until piece measures 14 (14, 14½, 14½ 15)"/35.5 (35.5, 37, 37, 38)cm from beg, end with a WS row.

Shape armholes

Bind off 5 (7, 9, 11, 13) sts at beg of next 2 rows. Dec 1 st each side every row 4 (5, 6, 7, 8) times—91 (97, 103, 109, 115) sts. Work even until armhole measures 7½ (8, 8½, 9, 9½)"/19 (20.5, 21.5, 23, 24)cm, end with a WS row.

Shape shoulders and neck

Bind off 9 (10, 10, 11, 12) sts at beg of next 2 rows, 8 (9, 10, 11, 12) sts at beg of next 2 rows, then 8 (9, 10, 11, 11) sts at beg of next 2 rows. AT THE SAME TIME, bind off center 21 (21, 23, 23, 25) sts, then bind off 5 sts from each neck edge twice.

Front

Work as for back until armhole measures 1½"/4cm, end with a WS row. Cont to shape armholes, if necessary, AT THE SAME TIME, work as foll:

Shape v-neck

Next row (RS) Work to center st, place center st on holder, join a 2nd ball of yarn, work to end. Working both sides at once, work next row even. Dec 1 st from each neck edge on next row, then every other row 19 (19, 20, 20, 21) times more— 25 (28, 30, 33, 35) sts each side. Work even until piece measures same as back to shoulder, end with a WS row. Shape shoulders as for back.

Sleeves

Cast on 57 (57, 59, 59, 61) sts. Work in k1, p1 rib for 1"/2.5cm, end with a WS row. Work in garter slip st for 1"/2.5cm, end with a WS row. Inc 1 st each side on next row, then every 10th (8th, 8th, 6th, 6th) row 2 (5, 13, 7, 13) times more, then every 12th (10th, 10th, 8th, 8th) row 10 (10, 4, 13, 9) times—83 (89, 95, 101, 107) sts. Work even until

piece measures 17 (17, 17½, 17½, 18)"/43 (43, 44.5, 44.5, 45.5)cm from beg, end with a WS row.

Shape cap

Bind off 5 (7, 9, 11, 13) sts at beg of next 2 rows. Dec 1 st each side every row 4 (6, 6, 8, 8) times, every other row 11 (12, 16, 20, 22) times, then every row 12 (10, 7, 2, 2) times—19 (19, 19, 19, 17) sts. Bind off knitwise.

Finishing

Block pieces to measurements. Sew shoulder seams.

Neckband

With RS facing and circular needle, beg at left shoulder seam and pick up and k 42 (44, 46, 48, 50) sts evenly spaced along left neck edge, place marker (pm), k1 from holder, pm, pick up and k 42 (44, 46, 48, 50) sts evenly spaced along left neck edge to right shoulder, pick up and k 37 (37, 39, 39, 41) sts evenly spaced across back neck—122 (126, 132, 136, 142) sts. Join and pm for beg of rnds.

Set-up rnd *K1, p1; rep from * to first marker, sl marker, k1, sl marker, *p1, k1; rep from *, end p1.

Next rnd Work in rib to 2 sts before first marker, k2tog, sl marker, k1, sl marker, ssk, work in rib to end. Rep last rnd 5 times more. Bind off all sts loosely in rib. Set in sleeves. Sew side and sleeve seams.

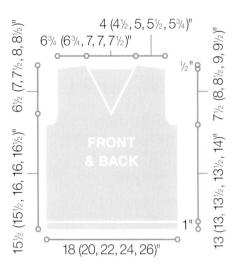

4 (4½, 5, 5½, 5¾)"
6¾ (6¾, 7, 7, 7½)"
½ "
6½ (7, 7½, 8, 8½)"
7½ (8, 8½, 9, 9½)"
FRONT & BACK
15½ (15½, 16, 16, 16½)"
13 (13, 13½, 13½, 14)"
1"
18 (20, 22, 24, 26)"

14 (15, 16, 17, 18)"
SLEEVE
4 (4¼, 4¾, 5¼, 5½)"
16 (16, 16½, 16½, 17)"
1"
9 (9, 9¼, 9¼, 9½)"

Guitar Sweater

Yarn 3

DK Weight Yarn
1¾ oz/50g skeins,
Each approx 115yd/105m
7 skeins in onyx
2 skeins in gold
1 skein each in bronze,
amethyst, and silver

Needles

One pair size 7 (4.5mm) knitting
needles or size to obtain gauge

Notions

Crochet hook size G/6 (4mm)
tapestry needle
stitch holder

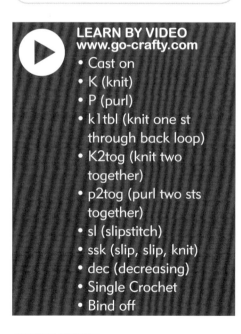

LEARN BY VIDEO
www.go-crafty.com
• Cast on
• K (knit)
• P (purl)
• k1tbl (knit one st through back loop)
• K2tog (knit two together)
• p2tog (purl two sts together)
• sl (slipstitch)
• ssk (slip, slip, knit)
• dec (decreasing)
• Single Crochet
• Bind off

Sized for S (M, L)

Measurements

Bust 34 (37, 40)"/86.5 (94, 101.5)cm
Length 24¼ (24¾, 25½)"/61.5 (63, 64.5)cm
Upperarm 13½ (14½, 15½)"/34.5 (37, 39.5)cm

Gauge

20 sts and 28 rows to 4"/10cm over St st using size 7 (4.5mm) needles. *Take time to check gauge.*

Note

When changing colors, twist yarns on WS to prevent holes in work. Make separate bobbins for each block of color. If desired, the strings of the guitar can worked in Duplicate stitch after pieces are knit, as were done in this sample. See page 54 for color workshop.

Front

With Onyx and size 7 (4.5mm) needles, cast on 86 (92, 100) sts. Work in k1, p1 rib for 5 rows. Beg with a purl row and work in St st for 3 rows.

Chart

(see pages 53 and 54)
Next row (RS) Beg and end as indicated, work in chart pat through row 100. Piece measures approx 15½"/39.5cm from beg.

Raglan Armholes and Neck

Work armhole shaping as shown on chart as follows: Bind off 2 sts at beg of next 2 rows—82 (88, 96) sts.
Row 1 (RS) K1, ssk, k to last 3 sts, k2tog, k1.
Row 2 P1, p2 tog, p to last 3 sts, p2tog tbl, p1.
Row 3 (RS) K1, ssk, k to last 3 sts, k2tog, k1.
Row 4 (WS) Purl all sts—76 (82, 90) sts.
Next row (RS) K1, ssk, k to last 3 sts, k2tog, k1.
Next row Purl. Repeat last two rows 22 (24, 27) times more, AT THE SAME TIME, on chart row 137 (141, 147), work neck shaping as foll:
Next row (RS) Bind off center 6 (8, 10) sts for neck and working both sides at

once, bind off from each neck edge 3 sts once, 2 sts once, dec 1 st every other row once, every 3 sts each side.

Back

With Onyx and size 7 (4.5mm) needles, cast on 86 (92, 100) sts. Work as for front with Onyx only (omitting chart pat) until same length as back to armhole.

Raglan Armholes and Neck

Work as for front, omitting neck shaping. After all armhole decreases have been worked, bind off rem 30 (32, 34) sts for back neck.

Sleeves

With Onyx and size 7 (4.5mm) needles, cast on 42 (42, 44) sts. Work in k1, p1 rib for 5 rows. Purl next row on WS, and cont in St st, inc 1 st each side every 8th (6th, 6th) row 8 (2, 8) times, every 10th (8th, 8th) row 5 (13, 9) times—68 (72, 78) sts. Work even until piece measures 18 (18½, 19)"/45.5 (47, 48) cm from beg.

Shape the Raglan Cap

Work same as back raglan armhole shaping. Bind off rem 12 sts.

Finishing

Block pieces to measurements. If desired, work strings in Duplicate st. Sew raglan sleeve caps to raglan armholes. Sew side and sleeve seams. With crochet hook and Onyx, work 1 round of single crochet edge evenly around neck opening.

Guitar Sweater

6 (6½, 6¾)"

7½ (8, 8¾)"

23 (23½, 24¼)"

15½"

17 (18½, 20)"

FRONT & BACK

7½ (8, 8¾)"

13½ (14½, 15½)"

18 (18½, 19)"

8½ (8½, 9)"

SLEEVES

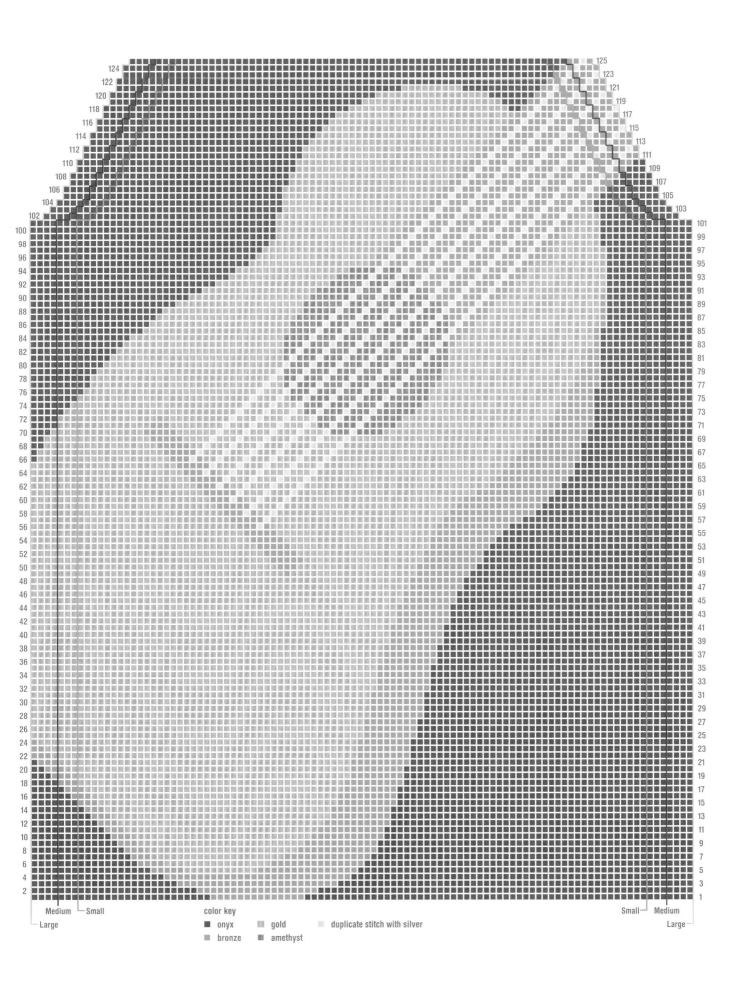

color key
onyx   gold   duplicate stitch with silver
bronze   amethyst

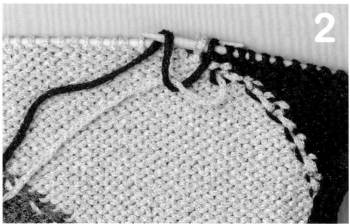

1 The next stitch is worked with black. Lay the gold yarn over top of the black.

2 Bring the black over top of the gold and purl the next stitch. Keep the floats neat, tugging the yarn a little (but not too much, or the fabric will pucker). A good tip: "Old color over new color."

3 After all the pieces have been knit, and before blocking and seaming, weave the extra ends into the wrong side. Thread the end into a tapestry needle, insert the needle into a loop near the end, then insert it into the next stitch in the opposite direction. Weave the strand in this way over several stitches, then cut it.

4 For small areas of color, embroider the stitches with duplicate stitch instead of knitting them in. Insert the tapestry needle from the back to the front in the center "V" of a stitch, then under the two loops of the same stitch one row above; pull through.

5 Insert the needle back into the center where the needle first came out to complete the stitch.

About Bobbins

  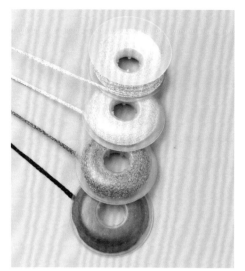

Make your own "butterfly" bobbins: hold the end of the yarn with your thumb. Wrap the yarn in a figure eight around your fingers as shown, then wrap the tail around the center and tie. Pull the yarn from the original tail.

Purchased bobbins, like the transparent ones shown above, prevent the different strands from getting tangled.

Baby Blanket

Yarn
Self-striping Chunky yarn
5oz/200g balls, each approx.
341 yd/312m (acrylic)
1 (2) balls in pink/orange/
yellow multi

Needles
One pair size 10 (6mm) needles
or size to obtain gauge

LEARN BY VIDEO
www.go-crafty.com
• Cast on
• Bind off

Measurements
• 23 x 24"/58.5 x 61cm
  (stroller version)
• 33 x 32"/84 x 81cm (crib version)

Gauge
16 sts and 18 rows to 4"/10cm over
basketweave pat using size 10 (6mm)
needles.
Take time to check gauge.

Basketweave Pattern
(multiple of 8 sts plus 6)
Row 1 (RS) K1, *k4, p4; rep from * to
last 5 sts, k5.
Rows 2–4 K the knit sts and p the
purl sts.
Row 5 K1, *p4, k4; rep from * to last
5 sts, p4, k1.
Rows 6–8 K the knit sts and p the
purl sts.
Rep rows 1–8 for basketweave pat.

Blanket
Cast on 94 (134) sts. Work in basketweave pat until 8 rows of pat have
been worked 13 (18) times, then work
rows 1–4 once (0) more for a total of
108 (144) rows. Piece measures approx
24 (32)"/61 (81)cm from beg. Bind off.